TAKE
the
TRIP!

**4 Journeys Every Midlife Woman Needs
To Live In Purpose and Freedom**

c.René Washington

DEDICATION

*To my parents: Barbara Ann Shoffner Williams,
my first life coach, and Abel Williams, Jr., who never
stopped believing I could fly.
I miss you daily.*

FOREWORD

What do you do when you are a middle-aged woman, dead in your once booming career, contemplating divorce after 20 years of marriage, being shattered by the untimely and unexpected death of your mother and having suffered a mini-stroke with no plausible explanation? The answer, my dear, is you take a trip!

Not your normal trip—a trip toward the abundant life that you know is out there waiting for you. A trip that will allow you to live in both purpose and freedom. This trip will consist of excursions to the islands of surrender, trust, love, and passion. During the trip, you will gain the keys that will empower you to surrender the "SHIT" that has held you back and down for far too long. You will learn to trust yourself and God more than the opinions of others. You will learn what true love is and how to recognize it when it comes knocking at your door. You will learn to embrace passion, and to not be afraid of it in your work, relationships and most importantly, in life. You will be able to distinguish the difference between happiness and joy and recognize why that is important. And finally, you will understand why pain is sometimes a necessary companion during the Journey to Surrender, Trust, Love and Passion.

c.René Washington, is a brilliant life coach, career advisor, world traveler, motivational speaker, scholar of life and my best friend. She is passionate and committed to helping midlife women who have sacrificed too much, too long and to the detriment of their personal well-being.

She has written this mini book so that she can touch as many women as possible who find themselves in the Valley of Not Enough. It is an easy but life changing read. I hope that it does for you, what it has done for me and countless other women who've found themselves living comfortable, attractive, but agonizingly unfulfilled lives. The best to each of you as you Reclaim, Redefine and Reinvent the lives you envisioned and now know that you deserve.

Sharon Sherrod
Best Friend and Grateful Traveler through my own journeys

INTRODUCTION

Four journeys inspired this book:

- My journey to surrender

- My journey to trusting myself

- My journey to loving myself

- My journey passion

So why is the book titled Take The Trip instead of Take The Journey? Because 'trip' has a dual meaning: traveling from one place to another and also stumbling along the way.

In the spring of 2019, I traveled solo to Lisbon Portugal. Originally planned as a trip with my husband I almost canceled when he was unable to go. Traveling thousands of miles to a place I'd never been seemed daunting. Then I remembered that a solo trip to Europe was on my *Be Brave* bucket list. I'm not a daredevil (or any kind of devil!) but once or twice a year, I try to do something that scares me. It staves off complacency and stimulates creativity. This certainly qualified and off I went for four revelatory days and nights. I returned home asking myself why I hadn't done this long ago?

Not long after, I took a much shorter trip to my favorite optical shop and there was a woman trying on two pairs of glasses, a red pair and a black pair.

"Get the red!" I said.
"Really?" she responded. "I like the red, but they're a little out there. My friends will talk about me."
"Yes, I said. They'll talk about how fabulous you look."

She went on to tell me that she'd been feeling like she was in a box. She used to be much more outgoing and there were so many things she'd been wanting to do, like travel, but hadn't. I told her that's exactly why she should get the red glasses. She'd be sending herself a message that "change gonna come" had arrived! I didn't wait around to see if she bought the red glasses. I hope she did buy them, and I hope you get your "red glasses" too.

Life is NOT over when you cross 50. Not by a long shot. We don't have to drop our hems, cut our hair and wear only black (I do love black, though!). Free your mind and your ass will follow! Shaking things up is good for your brain.

I'm guessing your inspiration to read this book (other than being related to me through blood or friendship) is coming from an inner whisper or an "Isn't there more to life?" nudging that won't leave you be. Say thank you! Because on the other side of your confusion, frustration, and F.E.A.R. (False Evidence Appearing Real) is the life you didn't believe was possible. A life full of transformational experiences, deep connections, laughter, joy, and delicious surprises. Releasing that F.E.A.R. got me to Lisbon and I hope it got that woman to wear the red glasses! *Take The Trip* is your ticket to fly to a Braver, Bolder, Best Life!

My Trip To Surrender

"You wanna fly, you got to give up the shit that weighs you down."

TONI MORRISON

~~~~~~~~~~

September 26, 2005, I took an unexpected and unwanted "trip" to the hospital. Some trips you plan (dream getaways) and some trips you don't! This was definitely one of those! But it took lying on a hospital gurney and being told you're having a major stroke to get crystal clear that what had been could no longer be.

At first, all I felt was shock. I drove myself to work that morning feeling some dizziness. The head nurse at my company was the one who sent me to the hospital with a TIA (mini-stroke) diagnosis. I just knew on arriving at the hospital that they would tell me she was mistaken. The dizziness and slurred nonsensical speech had ended. I felt normal again. By the time I was being transported to the ER, even the ambulance driver, made a (not) funny comment that I must simply want some time off work. But the hospital neurosurgeon agreed with the nurse and I was admitted for a five day stay of medication, tests and observation.

That wasn't my first hospital stay, but it was my first emergency stay. The first time I seriously considered death, or at least disability, a strong possibility if they couldn't prevent stroke.

They got my attention. More importantly, ultimately, I got *my* attention. I had no health triggers for stroke. I was only 45 years old. Wasn't overweight. No diabetes or high blood pressure. Two weeks before, I was diagnosed as being in full menopause, but hadn't taken enough medication to cause a stroke.

I knew the trigger, though: self-imposed stress from a deeply ingrained need to wear the mask of control, and from carrying the weight of obligated living and limiting beliefs. It was The Scream.

~~~~~~~~~~~~~~~

"Difficulties come when you don't pay attention to life's **whisper**. *Life always* **whispers** *to you* **first**, *but if you ignore the* **whisper**, *sooner or later you'll get a* **scream**"

OPRAH

~~~~~~~~~~~~~~~

As scared as being hospitalized was, I was also grateful for the reset. It was "permission" to focus only on me without explaining to anyone. It was "permission" to stop ignoring the whispers and examine The Scream.

Two days before the hospital trip, I was at my best friend's home with my (then) husband. I was pretending *Everything's All Right*, while feeling dejected and ungrateful. On paper, there was no reason for the emotional misery I was experiencing. All of the boxes were checked. Good man? Check. Good job? Check. Great family and friends? Check. Even my in-laws adored me!

All the ingredients for a great life, and for 20 years, life did feel great. Then, inexplicably, it no longer did. I felt boxed in, confused, and weighed down with a heaviness that I couldn't articulate. My overriding feeling was a need to escape. Leave my job, leave my marriage; disappear. And as we enjoyed a wonderful meal of food and laughter, all of these thoughts ran through me, but I convinced myself I had no socially acceptable reason to leave either. So, I made the decision to stay. Then, I began to weep.

Ending up on that hospital gurney two days after that dinner brought epiphany and decision: *Regardless of who understands, my marriage was over.*

And still, it took me another year to end the marriage. Six years to leave the corporate career. Thirteen years to completely trust God and myself without the filter of O.P.P. (Others' Paths and Perceptions). Thirteen years to stop externalizing and live from the inside out.

Surrendering is hard shit. My definition of surrender comes from author Tovah Silver in It's Not Your Money:

"Anything truly surrendered is made sacred. You're open and curious, surrendering to God showing you the way. You're not fixated on past regrets or a fantasy future. You learn to let everything that needs to go, go and let everything that needs to come, come."

3 Things I Know For Keeps

1. Suppression is unhealthy; possibly lethal. What's been suppressed, must be addressed. Stress constricts blood flow which constricts life flow.

2. Connecting to the root of stress, confusion, and frustration requires a lens turned inward. My husband didn't change. My job didn't change. I changed.

3. A decision is not a life sentence. We grow. We change. People and things may remain with you forever and they may not. Deciding on whom and what needs to go isn't about being selfish. It's about being self-*full*. Opening space to be full of whom and what lights you up. That puts you in the giving-even-more lane of life!

3 Ways You Can Avoid (or move past) The Scream

1. Acknowledge and prioritize dealing with what makes you wanna holla. Stop tripping over feeling guilty and selfish about your (secret) desires.

2. Let shit go. Declutter and Purge. If you're not already a fan of decluttering, you'll be amazed at the connection between releasing physical things and releasing internal clutter. I got rid of so much stuff, my new husband wondered when his "ass would be on the front lawn!"

3. Find an objective "safe-place" to share what's bubbling up. I don't tell everybody everything, but I have my front-row-girlfriend-crew whom I count on in the emotional clutch. Make sure you can trust them to keep it about you, not them. I've also gotten therapy and coaching. Keep testing until you find the one who works for you. I experienced a bad therapist but didn't stop looking for a good one.

RESOURCES

The Crossroads of Should and Must by Ella Luna
The Value In The Valley by Iyanla Vinzant
Growing Wings: The Power of Change at MarthaBeck.com
What I Know For Sure by Oprah Winfrey

What will you surrender? Fear? Control?
What will you release that sets you free?

~~~~~~~~~

_____

_____

_____

_____

_____

_____

_____

_____

_____

_____

_____

_____

_____

_____

_____

_____

_____

My Trip To Trusting Myself

"If I didn't define myself for myself, I would be crunched into other people's fantasies for me and eaten alive."

AUDRE LORDE

It was a great day at a local women's conference. I reconnected to old friends and former co-workers and listened to wonderfully inspiring speakers. So why was I walking to my car for the ride home in ugly-cry tears?

Because I kept running into women telling me how beneficial something I'd said or done had been for them. Yet, very few of those women had hired me. I'm a life coach and at that point in my entrepreneurial journey, my success had been up and down, and I was exhausted. Even though I could check off a long list of women's lives changed through my coaching, from a business perspective, I felt like a failure. I decided that I was DONE! I tucked my tail and went into full pity-party mode for a whole month.

Although I was down, I wasn't completely out. I'm a mindset coach and I do drink my own tea. Mindset work centers around examining your internal messaging. What stories are you telling yourself? What are you making something mean? Is that true? Thoughts lead to feelings. Feelings lead to actions. And actions lead to results/consequences.

I know that I'm an excellent coach, but at the end of the conference, I told myself I was a terrible businesswoman(thought). And that made me feel like crap, hence the ugly-cry meltdown(feelings). And that led me to go into the fetal position shut down (action). Hiding from my business. No blogs, client outreach, or marketing (consequences).

While I am a life-coach, I am also a woman of strong Christian faith and the daughter of two of the strongest people to have walked the planet. In weak moments, I get in the mirror and speak out loud, "I am Barbara Ann's daughter and a Child of The Most High God!" I can hear my mom saying, "René, get up!" and my dad saying, "Girl get yourself together." So, I did.

And when I got up, the assessment began. I landed on Seth Godin's book, *The Dip: A Little Book That Teaches You When To Quit (and When to Stick)*. I love the topic of quitting. We're taught to "never quit". To finish a thing to the bitter end, no matter how miserable it makes you. I totally reject this. I ascribe to Beyoncé's version of quitting: "A winner never quits on HERSELF!" Sticking with something you hate requires more energy. At times, it can be downright exhausting. In addition to that, sticking to something you hate blocks space for your *better* and blocks space for the person to step in who would actually love it. I mentioned leaving a 21-year marriage and career in the Surrender chapter. What I didn't share is that I left my career five years before official retirement. Both decisions were extremely difficult, and both were "never-regret" decisions. Was ending my business going to join them on the "quit" list?

Godin defines *the Dip* as "the long slog between starting and mastery." He says that during that slog, *the Dip* of wanting to give up will come and only a small percentage will push through to mastery and success.

When I took the true view of myself, I hadn't been in the game long enough to achieve mastery AND I'd been bopping from business coach to business coach, trying this sure-fire plan then the next one; mostly leaving me frustrated and overwhelmed. I was also taking work that I didn't enjoy. That ended up in an epic-fail that almost cost me a deeply important friendship. I'd fallen into the very same trap that I coach clients through: Not listening to my inner compass. As Aunt Vi said in the tv show, *Queen Sugar*, "Girl you need to come back to yourself." (If ya'll aren't watching Queen Sugar, you need to fix that!) I'd drowned out my inner truth voice with a cacophony of experts.

There's rarely only one way to do anything. I'm a huge fan of books, courses, and coaching (remember, I'm a tea drinker) and what my *Dip* reminded me is that all information needs to first be filtered through our inner-knowing of what works for us. The business coaches were great, but I needed to clear out mindshit and be absolutely grounded in and aligned with my *Who Am I*. Turns out, I had blocks around worthiness and money.

I began separating the wheat from the chaff, keeping business practices that work for me and ditching those that don't. I did deep work on my blocks with two money-mindset coaches. I stopped being afraid to try things (a podcast) and make big pivots (a partnership).

Now, I surrender to God's will and trust my inner compass to follow that will. Business is consistently *poppin'* and I'm having fun. The business pivot I took was starting a career coaching partnership with two brilliant women. It's taken off in a big way, providing opportunities to help even more women. I contract with other coaches to coach in their businesses and I still do individual coaching with women in mid-life transition. And in a full circle moment: the women's conference where I had my meltdown asked me back a few years later to present on the main stage! Instead of doing it solo, I pitched the partnership and we had an amazing time. This is not about running a business. It's about allowing yourself to connect to YOUR THING and trusting yourself to do it.

I no longer question my intuition/body compass/inner knowing/gut feeling/first right mind/spiritual gps. I simply trust it.

3 Things I Know For Keeps

1. *Knowing Who You Are* at core-level (without role or title) keeps you laser focused and aligned with Hell yesses! or Hell no! decisions.

2. My faith in God grounds and sustains my belief in myself. You may not follow a particular religion but having faith in something higher than yourself allows for way out of no-way miracles.

3. Yes, the shortest distance between two points is a straight line, but the scenic route often provides a harvest of abundance lessons. Don't be afraid of the dips and detours. Mine have connected me to some of the most amazing people and experiences.

Nothing is wasted!

3 Ways You Can Come Out Of Your Dip

~~~~~~~~~

1. Do your *Who Am I?* work. Get crystal clear on what YOU (sans filter and obligation) wants, and *Own It*!

2. *Let Shit Go!* I know I sound like a broken record, but from a physiological perspective, holding onto shit is at minimum, uncomfortable and at most debilitating. It's the same for mindshit. Did you know that it takes five positive messages to overwrite one negative message? Engage in a daily mindset reset practice: prayer, meditation, affirmations, books, podcasts, etc.

3. Document intuitive decisions (no matter how small) for a month to see proof that no one knows better for you than you!

RESOURCES

The Dip: A Little Book That Teaches You When To Quit (and When to Stick) by Seth Godin
The Year of Yes by Shonda Rhimes
The Big Leap by Gay Hendricks
Oprah & Deepak 21-Day Meditations
Podcast *Therapy For Black Girls*
Podcast *Midlife Woman Redefined (the first season of my podcast!)*
Money mindset coaches: *Mary Houston, Keisha Dixon*

Who are you without role or title?
Drop old narratives that no longer serve you
and journal the new story of You.

~~~~~~~~~~~~~~

_____

_____

_____

_____

_____

_____

_____

_____

_____

_____

_____

_____

_____

_____

_____

My Trip To Loving Myself

"Woke up this morning with my mind...set on loving me."
FROM SONG, "HOLY" BY JAMILA WOODS

A few years ago, I had a life-altering conversation with a horse named Ireland. That the conversation even occurred was amazing in and of itself. I was in Savannah, Georgia, with a group of women going through a week-long certification to become a BARE coach. BARE is Susan Hyatt's "never diet again" path to treating yourself with love in all areas of your life and ditching a lot of weight (mental, emotional and physical). Included in the certification process was a day at a horse farm for Equus Coaching. I AM NOT AN ANIMAL PERSON. Our Equus Coach, Shepard Lake, met with us the night before to explain what would happen. More than once, she told us that if our horse got skittish, it could kick us in the head and kill us. *Hellllll Na!* That sealed it for me! I would go, but only to cheer my sister coaches from the sidelines.

It was a lovely, sunshiny day. The farm had the cutest baby goats and majestic horses. I watched the other women step into their power by leading those beautifully magnificent creatures around a ring, while sharing their desires and fears with them. Still determined not to do it, I started feeling a twinge that maybe I could reconsider. Shepard checked in periodically with me, but there was no pressure from her or Susan to do it. My NO resolve wavered. Then Shepard gave me an alternative. Instead of leading the horse around the ring, I could stand by him and have my conversation while she stood nearby. Plan!

In speaking to Ireland as if he were my better self, I said:
"Dear René, I'm so grateful for the fears you've helped me face: fear of making my business successful. Fear of failing. I no longer have to keep wondering if I'm on the right path: I Am. I know what my Emerald City looks like. You are TOTALLY CHILL in your bigness and I can be too. Running a business is hard and that's ok. I can stop making it harder than it is. Simply stop. Like you did when you decided to talk to me. Now you know that when you need help, you can get it. Thank you René (Ireland)!"

I pushed through fear and nobody died.

I wrote these words down and periodically, I'll pull them out as a reminder. I no longer get on scales unless at a doctor's office. The only weight I track is the internal weight I need to release. Women can be in complicated and constantly fluxing relationships with our bodies. I went from a teenager wanting my parents to buy me the weight-on product from the *Soul Train* commercials so I could be hips-and-breasts-fine to a grown-ass woman who's daily question to my husband was: "Does this make my butt look TOO big?" Have mercy!

BARE not only helped me realize how body perception influences who we are and what we do, it also validated what I suspected: the traditional deprivation playbook feeds a life of constricting and limiting what we believe we deserve.

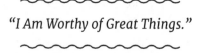

"I Am Worthy of Great Things."

This quote is on my bathroom mirror and I repeat it out loud every day, butt naked. Not only do I see myself differently, I see other women differently. How much would we weigh if we carried all of our internal shit as physical weight? Weight is a number that tells me very little about a person. My weight tells you very little about me.

Treating myself with love translates into:

- Refusing to own anyone else's definition of me.

- Eating with intention and attention to what my body loves and feels good consuming.

- Eating on beautiful dishes daily.

- Moving in ways that support health and flexibility.

- Feeding my mind, spirit, and soul level up nourishment through media and relationships.

- Only wearing clothes that make me feel fly and beautiful.

- Adding as much pleasure, fun, and joy in my life as possible!

What I Know For Keeps

~~~~~~~~~~~~~~~~~~

1. Every day is a new day to love the skin I'm in.

2. Every day is a new day to love the body I'm in.

3. Every day is a new day to do the great things and
be the great things, because I'm worthy.

3 Ways You Can Learn To Love Yourself

1. Decide today that you deserve the love you give to everyone else.

2. Speak self-love into your mirror every day out loud. Extra credit for doing it naked. It will feel weird at first, but keep doing it. I promise it makes a difference!

3. Treat yourself to the BARE book by Susan Hyatt and follow the path to self-love.

RESOURCES

BARE by Susan Hyatt
Follow *GirlTrek.org*, radical self-care and healing through walking
Listen to Rachel Rodgers' podcast, *Hello Seven* (even if you don't want to start a business, you'll want to treat yourself like a million bucks)
Create a *Love Yourself* playlist. Start with the Estelle/Janelle Monae song, *Do My Thing.*

One of my favorite 'loving myself' exercises is from BARE. Gaze at yourself in the mirror (preferably full length) while naked. Express gratitude for each part of your body, giving extra attention to the parts you've been telling yourself you hate. Journal your gratitude for every inch. Commit to giving up disparaging self-talk.

~~~~~~~~~~~

My Trip To Passion

"There is no passion to be found playing small...in settling for a life that is less than the one you are capable of living."

NELSON MANDELA

I've always loved celebrating birthdays. I've always been excited about getting older. I remember our high school band director telling my senior class that high school years would be the best years of our lives. *Helllllll to the NA NA NA!!!!!* That was NOT going to be true for me. When I was a few years away from turning 50, my excitement ratcheted up even higher because I deemed 50: the Queen Coronation of birthdays. In my mind, if you didn't have your life together by 50, life was a wrap!

I celebrated that milestone for 18 months:

- Went to the Oprah show twice.
- Had an Eat Dessert First party with enough sweets to stock a small store.
- Hosted a girlfriends beach weekend.
- Did a mom and daughter road trip to Savannah to tour historic homes.
- Fell in love again.
- Whatever caught my fancy, turning 50 was the permission.

Living life well has always been high priority for me, but after turning 45 and going through a mini-stroke, a divorce, and menopause, fear started to creep in about how much longer I had to be on this earth. So, I was in say-yes-to-everything mode, wanting to reach the holy grail of 50, then coast on out for however many years remained. I ended my 50th birthday celebration marathon the day before I turned 51, with a New Orleans-style Second Line Parade! My family and girlfriends dance-strutted around a local park with me, led by three musicians playing "Do Whatcha Wanna" (Rebirth Brass Band). Epically fun! A woman in a high-rise across the street saw us from her balcony and ran over to join us. It was the best! The night ended with us enjoying a fancy dinner at the Hot & Hot Fish Club. It was truly a cloud 9 entry into a decade that turned out to be, not an ending, but the beginning of the best of times and worst of times years.

I kicked off the fifties in high-style and was newly in-love. Talk about grand passion. The depth of feeling I felt for this man who dropped into my life was revelatory and scary. I was used to being in control and at the same time it was I-can-exhale exciting to be with a man who can plan and execute and still respect my independence. We were flying high...literally. He was still working in New York City and we became the poster couple for making long-distance-love work.

Two years later, I was in a meeting. My sister (we were at the same company) interrupted the meeting to tell me our mom had fallen. My parents lived about 70 miles away and we jumped in the car with my fiancé to go to the hospital. We laughed and talked during the drive and at one point I asked my sister if she'd heard anything else from our dad. She responded, no and we kept chatting. When we arrived at the hospital and asked for Mom's room number, we were led down a hall, totally clueless until a door to a small room was opened and we saw Dad standing there looking as if all the blood had drained from his body. There was another man standing with him and we instantly knew: Mom was dead. She'd had a pulmonary embolism and they couldn't revive her. It was October 5th, 2011. The word "shock" doesn't come close to describing how we and really everyone who knew her felt.

I could write an entire book on the amazing woman my mom was and will instead sum it up with this: Apple founder, Steve Jobs and civil rights activist Fred Shuttlesworth both died the same day Mom did and she was as impactful in the lives of the people who knew her as they were to the world. *Life is short* was one of my mantras, but after her death, it changed to *life is arbitrary*. I began paying close attention to who lived and who died because her death was so unexpected; so unfair. My biggest "unfair" example? The Rolling Stones. Not because I want them to be dead, but because I can't believe that with all the drugs, women, and road rockin' they've done, they're still alive! And doing concerts! Mick survived heart surgery at age 75, then went on tour!! My mom was a vibrant 74 when she died. Or I'd see a story like the couple in an SUV who were hit from behind while stopped at a traffic light, both killed instantly. In an SUV. Arbitrary!

I had mainly focused on life being fun. Being a good person and living a nice life. After Mom's death, I wanted to be much more intentional. To work IN purpose, ON purpose. I was still in corporate and becoming more and more miserable, trying to hold out until official retirement at age 55. Robert would say that it started raining in the house on Sunday evenings because I dreaded going to work on Mondays. I prayed continuously for a new attitude or a release. I got the release.

First was the mindset reset. Most people externalize misery, and I was no exception. Staying focused on the company being the source of my unhappiness blocked my seeing what was really going on. I'd complain to Robert that I didn't understand why God

43

wasn't answering my 'help me stay' prayers. His response was Glenda The Good Witch worthy: "Maybe God's packing your bags."

Bam! That coupled with realizing that it wasn't about the job changing. It was about me changing. The company had revised the retirement criteria three times during my tenure. Why was I letting arbitrarily chosen criteria determine my life's trajectory? I GET TO CHOOSE. I chose starting a new chapter.

A year after Mom's death and three years before being eligible for retirement, I left my 27-year career with no plan for what was next. I'd fallen in love with a man who cracked open dormant passion in me that I didn't even know I was missing and I believed that passion would fuel a new season of purpose and passion in continuing to pour into the lives of others.

~~~~~~~~~~

"When you do something from your soul, you feel a river moving in you, a joy."

RUMI

~~~~~~~~~~

3 Things I Know For Keeps

1. Burnout is a sign to look within. Most of my corporate years were wonderfully successful and impactful. The ending burnout was simply a push to break out of a box that no longer fit and level up my life's impact.

2. Our life perspective is a choice. We have a birth date and there will be a death date. My focus remains on how I'm living the dash in between.

3. Being multi-passionate is not the same as multi-tasking. I'm passionate about many things: my faith, Mr. Washington, coaching women, books, the arts, social justice, girlfriend gatherings, yummy desserts, travel, trees, dancing, and more.

4 Ways To Tap Into Your Passion

- Read *The Crossroads* and *Should and Must* by Ella Luna (Recommended twice because I love it so much as a path to passion and antidote to complacency).

- Fire up ALL of your senses. Really smell the flowers or the coffee. Cuddle with your boo, pet, baby. Paint, draw, sing, dance, cook, etc.

- Incorporate DAILY pleasure as ritual (see the BARE book). Two examples for me: I upgraded my tuna and those sandwiches are a WHOLE 'nother level of yum! Time on our patio, watching trees sway, birds flitter, talking to hubby or simply being chill.

- Get help getting out of your own way! Ditch your shit through therapy. Move forward working with a great life coach (I may be biased, but for the worried well, I believe there's no better path than coaching to closing the gap between where you are and where you want to be).

RESOURCES

Find a Therapist *Therapy For Black Girls,*
https:// therapyforblackgirls.com
Find a Coach *The International Coaching Federation,*
https://coachfederation.org/credentialed-coach-finder
Find a Coach: *Ask me! I know amazing coaches for marriage, business, nutrition/healthy living, money mindset, sex and intimacy, entrepreneurship, and more. Send your questions to Rene@cReneCoach.com.*
Keep a More Please journal: *when something lights you up, write it down to remember the experience AND to repeat it!*

Let it all rip here! Journal your secret/not so secret desires, your cravings, all the things that light you up. From small daily pleasures to epic adventures. Hold nothing back whether or not you believe it's possible. God loves busting our impossibility beliefs.

~~~~~~~~~~~~~~

_____

_____

_____

_____

_____

_____

_____

_____

_____

_____

_____

_____

_____

Wouldn't Take Nothing For My Journeys

"What you're supposed to do when you don't like a thing is change it. If you can't change it, change the way you think about it. Don't complain."

MAYA ANGELOU

Surrender. Trust. Love. Passion. These journeys are layered, but not linear, tripping in and out of the complexities of happiness, joy, and pain. I've learned to divorce from a specific outcome and stay grounded in faith in God's will for my life. Every mental block and limiting belief I release opens up space for new amazingness. And that continuous release from what keeps me stuck, from moving forward, from living in purpose, from experiencing every good thing is the lifelong journey.

However you get there, *Let Shit Go* and get there! I shared my journeys for the women who are not satisfied with hiding on the sidelines of their lives. You believe that life is to be lived until the very last drop.

I share these journeys for the women who want to buy the red glasses, but are afraid of being judged.

I share these journeys for the women like my client who was mentally and physically exhausted from being everyone's go-to, volunteer, listening ear, one-way street. She was ready to not only be on her priority list, but be at the top of it. After working through her *Who Am I?* and owning her new story about herself: *It's my time and I'm ready to give myself, Yes-to-Me permission*, she made major life changes. Her son moved out. She let go of "stayed too long" volunteer commitments. She said NO, without explanation, when asked to keep a friend's child on an evening she'd planned for *Me Time*. Those small wins led to her quitting her job and moving three states away to start a new chapter living near her grandchildren and helping with their care.

I share these journeys for the women like my client who left her good government job to start a private law practice. Or the women like my client who left her corporate career to focus on the charitable foundation she created. Or the women like my client who made peace with carving out time to take an international trip while still being committed to caregiving responsibilities.

Fifty wasn't an ending. It was the beginning of coming into the fullness of the flow and glow years. And I turnt UP for my entry into the sixties:

- Taking my first international solo to Lisbon, Portugal.

- Starting a podcast (Midlife Woman Redefined)

- Two weeks in France and Morocco with 12 girlfriends (we call ourself The VIVAs) that included visiting Josephine Baker's chateau (in a flapper dress!) and another Second Line Parade. This time across the Seine River, with a live band who adored us!

- Starting a new business with two besties (CareerTriageHQ.com)

Let the shit go that's holding you back from your dreams, your desires, your passion and purpose. Answer that nudge that keeps calling you. I pray passionately fulfilling and joyful journeys for you!

The Final What You Can Do

If you take anything from this book let it be:

- Stop self-defeating messaging...Ta-DAY! Feed yourself "Yes, I Can" messaging everyday. Now that this is a focus, I see positive messaging everywhere...on buildings, in the street, on clothing. Everywhere. It's true, your focus calls in more of what you focus on. So, make it good.

- Translate "Yes, I Can" messaging into feel the fear and do it anyway action. If you need professional help doing this, invest in yourself. Remember, you're worthy!

Resources

Do you have a personal femifesto? It's the more accurate tag for a woman's manifesto. And it's a lovely way to remind yourself of yourself. Google manifestos for templates and see mine below.

MY FEMIFESTO

I'm c.René, a woman who lives life on and in purpose, fully committed to moving in personal freedom, loving deeply and helping other women do the same.

I do the work to keep letting my shit go:
the old and false beliefs that don't serve me...
that keep me stuck...

F.E.A.R. (false evidence appearing real)...
mental and physical clutter...
unhealthy habits...
guilt for FINALLY putting myself first...
criticism and judgement of self and others.

I lovingly call B.S. when I see myself falling into the above traps. I do ALL the things to keep myself encouraged and focused on what I CAN DO then DOING IT!

I respect my past yet refuse to be stuck in it.

I focus on creating new stories...taking bold action that moves me into the life I want to manifest.

I've...
    gone through some things,
    done things I shouldn't have done,
    gone places I shouldn't have gone,
    said some things I shouldn't have said.

I'm perfectly imperfect and I walk in the divine perfection of the grace and mercy of multiple chances from The Most High God. And I've learned to extend the grace I want to receive.

I am forgiven. I forgive myself.

My life moves forward through desire. I reclaim my dreams... my life.

This is my time.

Loving myself opens me up to MORE, not less. To become self-FULL, not selfish. To drop the weight of false obligation and inauthenticity and to...

Get Real. Be Real. Live and Love On Purpose....In Purpose.
Finally, this book was written in the midst of health, financial, and racial pandemics. More and more women are amplifying their voices and stepping into higher levels of leadership to be a part of creating new paradigms. Be one of those women! Find your lane and step into it.

DO THIS...

~~~~~~~~~~~~~~~~

Write your own femifesto...your commitment to living your best life.

_____

_____

_____

_____

_____

_____

_____

_____

_____

_____

_____

_____

_____

_____

_____

_____

_____

ACKNOWLEDGMENT

I am so very blessed in my village! Thank you doesn't fully cover my gratitude to...

Robert Washington, Jr., my husband, life love, and Grown-Ass-Man. You get me and you've got me. You keep me flowing in laughter, Perrier water and ice cream. Your unwavering support of my dreams takes my breath away.

My sister, Romelia, brother-in-love, Roy, and nieces, Brittany and Sydney. You always show up. Always.

Aunt Pat and Cousin Barbara. You showed me in very different ways how to stand in my truth.

The VIVAs. You're my besties, prayer warriors, travel buddies and the women who fully exemplify the awesomeness of friend-ship and fabulosity!

My mentor coaches: Lee Irwin Sumner, Susan Hyatt, Rachel Rodgers, Keisha Dixon, and Mary Houston. You helped me let my shit go.

Sister coaches. I'm a lifelong learner and serial course taker, and the bonus is always connecting to forever-friends who are also on the heroine's journey. The value you've added to my life is incalculable.

Clients. The women I work with have been such a gift! Thank you for trusting me on your journeys.

Writing coaches Alexandra Franzen and Lindsey Smith. You make what feels impossible, not only possible, but DONE! Thank you for getting me to the published-author finish line.

Everyone else who's sent a kind thought, spoken an encouraging word. Thank you!!

Finally, but not least, I'm sending up a hallelujah shout out for God's grace and path clearing in reaching this goal. Thank you, Jesus!